Toilet Feelings

Igoe Brown

Published by Igoe Brown, 2024.

TOILET FEELINGS

First edition. November 25, 2024.

ISBN: 979-8230710950

Written by Igoe Brown.

Table of Contents

To all those that feel less than, know you are enough.

A Toilet Feeling isn't exactly a toilet feeling

Toilet Feelings aren't just for the toilet
They could be anywhere

    at work
    on the bus
    at the grocery store
    at the library
    in bed
    at your parent's house
    at the doctor's office
    in job interviews
    on dating sites
    during therapy
    in the mirror
    on a walk
    at church
    walking past the church
    in the voting booth
    at weddings
    at funerals
    at the family Thanksgiving dinner
    in the kitchen making dinner
    or breakfast
    while playing video games
    while reading a book
    during a date
    while housesitting
    while on vacation
    on the subway in a different city
    in strange toilets

   in familiar toilets
   in strange toilets that at this point should be familiar

It's a feeling
It's being alone
Even if you're not *alone* alone
It's the terrible feelings that need to be flushed away forever
But your body will always make more of
The ones we all have
But some of us have Pee Pee Problems that make it worse

Back and More Messed Up than Ever

I've missed this.
Us.
Being alone with myself
and sharing with myself
What needs to be expressed.

Four years ago,
the depression took away my voice
my ability to speak.
But somehow I was able to write.

Then I could barely do either.

Now I can read again!
I'm reading poetry again too,
going to reading groups,
Sharing my thoughts and feelings about writing.

Now I want to share my thoughts and feelings through writing again
too.

Alone in the Toilet

Toilet toilet toilet
Instead of talking
I have to spend time in the toilet

I haven't been doing my kegel stretches
And I have my appointment next week

Why do I always have these Toilet Feelings after club?

Now I have no one to talk to
about how club went
to help soothe these Toilet Feelings

I'm grabbing the trash can
so something other than words
can come out of my mouth

The toilet is a closet
Where I don't have to be seen
All my secrets can be hidden here
My scars and my pee

I don't have to face

    anyone
     or anything

All my stress waits outside the door
As I sit and ruminate

Feeling like a piece of shit while I shit
The toilet room
Alone again
I'll be alone again when I get home
Or there with Not Friends

My world's on fire, how bout yours?

Wynn Bruce setting himself on fire on the Supreme Court steps on Earth day 2022 at 6:30pm

People drowned sleeping in basement apartments during a dying hurricane
People dead from heat with broken ACs
Or frozen to death in Houston with prices gouged

Prisoners dying while fighting fires for slave wages
Dying at Rikers from COVID because they didn't set your court date yet
Scientists getting arrested publicly demanding a defunding of fossil fuels on the steps and gates of national government buildings and the doors of JP Morgan Chase

Indigenous bodies on the front lines stopping pipelines while we find thousands of indigenous children's bodies in the ground

What is the point of anything if not to be a water protector?

Our cries are so loud but ignored and 2°C is looming

Louisiana is underwater and Ferguson still doesn't have clean water
Our communities are polluted;

    I drink lead water at work
    there was asbestos falling from my public school's ceiling

40 migrants dead from heat exhaustion. Abandoned.
15 Kentuckians dead from flooding. Numbers expected to double as search continues.
A Palestine in Ohio is burning, adding acid to the air.

David Buckle had self immolated in Prospect Park at 6:30am April 14, 2018

B. C. Before Corona

The before times
When we had slow news days
When your dollar went farther
When we didn't know the compassion levels of our neighbors and our
communities

Before the isolation
Before all the shots and the masks
Before the fear

    the loss

When people knew what my face looked like
When my brother was still a child

    still straight
    before we were the same

When we still got trick or treaters
When abolishing the police was a radical idea

Before George Floyd
Before Wynn Bruce
Before the insurrection
Before Qanon
Before my blood clots
Before
Before
Before

We can't go back to before

Are these things worth saying

    Worth sharing

Who will read them
What will they say
Somehow I know what they will speak
Will be worth saying

But myself

My little toilet bowl
All mine
Carved from stolen stone
What I write here is all my own

He says I shouldn't feel bad about what I said

    They were my feelings

But *he* said who was harmed

I was harmed

I can only say it here
In my little bowl
All my own

You see I *have* changed my name

    (Here again a different one lies)

It isn't my fault you cannot recognize it

There isn't any more I should do to demand respect and dignity

I don't need to hand out hundreds of dollars to a government that

    doesn't recognize me
    owes me money
    serves the elites
    instead of its poor transgender children

I don't need to *get fingerprinted*

    as though I'm doing something illegal
    as though *I'm* illegal

I don't need the government to have a record of my transgender status

    or *anyone* else's

I don't need to publicize, more than I already have, so far and so wide
that it even reaches those irrelevant that I am transgender

You don't have to do anything to have me call you by *your* chosen name

What is the shape of a man

Two beings in the shape of men

I know cisgender men that

> have large breasts
> do not have testicles
> have small or altered dicks
> cannot grow beards
> have high pitched voices, singing soprano
> are lithe and flexible
> are curvy
> wear makeup and paint their nails
> are excellent dancers
> are the biggest gossips
> giggle
> cry
> are very affectionate
> are soft
> care for others
> are homemakers
> like to shop
> have skin care routines
> prefer to bottom
> don't eat meat
> shave their legs
> use hormone therapy

What is the shape of a man?

Your name is my passcode for most things
No matter the ways in the past you've hurt me

    in the ignorance of youth

I love you immeasurably

The distance is difficult
As you carve out a life for yourself in a new city
And I contemplate moving myself father away from you

I have an older poem about a toilet
it's not very good
it's not worth sharing

But it's not new to have my life shaped by the toilet
One aliment ends and is followed by another

I was 15 and at peak menstrual pain
My undiagnosed fibroid causing clot after clot to fall into the toilet
Causing chronic debilitating pain
Causing me to throw up
Causing me to faint

I spent a great deal of time in my adolescence in the bathroom
Needing to know where a bathroom was at all times

In adulthood I have the added issue of not knowing what bathroom I
could use
Should use
What all gender bathroom was available to me

But there I was
Trying not to pass out on the toilet
Blood steadily dripping out of me
And cold sweat dripping down me

I was so focused on what was happening to me
That when two girls entered the bathroom
I groaned for a different reason

I just wanted to be alone
I wanted privacy

And all they were talking about was *boys*
In my idiocy of my youth I wrote that their conversation didn't pass the
Bechdal Test

But then one of the girls mentioned her pregnancy
And all my problems felt small
In comparison to a complete shift in life
My toilet problems are chronic
Hers were short term
But would change the trajectory of her life

There we all were in the girls bathroom that all the afab weird, hairy,
queer, and students of color had to change in for theatre
Because there wasn't enough room for us with the normal skinny white
cishet girls
And I was ditching gym class to die on the toilet
And they were ditching their classes to talk about a pregnancy
Separated by the stall doors

A half court
At an apartment complex
Across the street from my therapist's office

I'm sitting at the bus stop with my groceries
And the only thing in my immediate line of sight
Are these four children

Boys against girls
All wearing their team colors
The smallest among them seems the most skilled
I can hear their cries when they get the ball in the hoop

My nerves unfurl from my body like a growing bloom
Reaching out to demonstrate different shapes and colors it can take
But they all have the same roots

    This blossom of self doubt
    That bud of negative body image
    The branch of low self esteem

All have deep roots sprouted from the seeds of neglect

A morning ruined
All over a phone call

Thank you for your professionalism

All those social bonds

>cut
>with just a few words

Staring out the window at 1am

What fills this emptiness
This lack of

    fulfillment
    meaning

in my life

When do I feel whole
When do I feel complete
When do these

    minutes
    hours
    days
    months
    years

Begin to mean something

1. Stop looking at your phone
2. Brush your teeth
3. Wash your face
4. Fill your CPAP machine up with water so you're not so thirsty you're gonna die at 1am
5. Stop looking at your phone
6. Change into your jammies if you haven't already
7. Select your bedtime buddy, may I offer Cookie Monster or Roscoe the non-binary raccoon? Perhaps Hello Kitty?
8. Apply chapstick, also helps with CPAP dryness
9. Turn out all lights, expect for bedside lamp
10. Pull back the covers and get into bed
11. Finally look at your phone to set up your alarm for the morning, then plug in to charge
12. Turn on white noise
13. Apply eczema cream so you're moisturized for the night
14. Take off glasses
15. Put on CPAP face mask
16. Turn off bedside lamp
17. And curl up in bed
18. Try to keep the bad thoughts away
19. Stop looking at your phone

I'm trying to flush these Toilet Feelings down
One after the other
Get rid of them!
So I can sleep

But it's too much
It's overflowing
They're all coming back up

An Ant on the Bus

An ant on the bus
Crawling around the seats and dividers
What a tragic and beautiful thing

Going farther than any of your community

    seeing the world

How will you get back to them?
How will you live on your own?
Will you find another hill to live in?
Will someone knowingly or unknowingly squash you?

    (Like I squashed the spotted lanternfly)
    (INVASIVE SPECIES)

How did you get to be on the bus? Who let you on without paying a
fare?
Where are you going?
Which is your stop?
Do you need me to pull the rope?

When will you get home?
When will any of us get home?

Can anyone see behind my sunglasses?
Can they see the tears getting soaked up by my mask?
Can they hear me suck up my snot?
Can anyone tell I'm falling apart?

I sit on the toilet
Devoid of distractions
Alone with my thoughts
Peeing

You're ugly
Why are you doing this?
No one loves you

I sit down and my self esteem goes with it

I'm finishing up peeing and the toilet begins to gurgle

> I purposely chose this stall because the other one was clogged

I wipe and stand up
The toilet automatically flushes
I bend over to pull up my underwear and the toilet gurgles again

The water splashes out and sucks me in
Down and down and down its pipes
I'm tossed around corners and pass intersections
All the way down
Down to the dark underground
The utter bottom of my self esteem
Surrounded by all my failings

Every mistake
Every blemish
Every outburst and flashback
Every bad hair day
Every time I've gained weight

It's a showcase of my pathetic life
I walk around the displays
Unlike the museum I can touch

> But I'd rather not

The most recent incidents are prominently displayed

All of my coworkers' comments

    You ask too many questions
    You're trying to help and you're making it worse

I'm stuck staring at the purples and blues and throw up yellow-green
Overcome and ashamed
Cannibalizing my own shame
Like the ouroboros

Finally able to pull away
I walk past smaller less recent offenses

    From my youth
    From school
    From church

They all blend together
They do not stand out
But the feelings they portray are thick

Then there are the largest displays

    of my family

The shame is cold

    and crushing

    You were a miserable child
    You're setting a bad example for your brother
    You shouldn't be doing that

Why can't you be like your brothers

...
I'm running
Running away from them
From these feelings
There's no escape
So I start climbing the wall
Needing to get out

The dirt turns to metal pipes
I have no water to push me
so I must pull myself up against gravity
I go for miles
counting the pipes by tens

After a turn I see light
There is water again
I crawl out into my toilet at home
I keep going to my room
To shut out the world
In my own private toilet bowl

Drifting in this sea of toilet feelings
I don't remember where I begin or end
I don't remember what my body

    looks like
    feels like
    is shaped like

If I were to die here in the bathroom no one would know
My blood sucked right out of my cuts

    (no clotting with my anticoagulants)

My body would be treated like a goldfish
I'll be flushed down the bowl and that would be all
The sea will dry up and be replaced with another

Bereft
Afloat
Adrift
Somewhere else
Trying to get
Somewhere else

Alone alone alone
Always alone

    We're born alone

    We live alone

    We die alone

    Only through our love and friendship can we create the illusion for the moment that we're not alone

    -Wells

This cruel cruel world capitalizes and thrives on our loneliness
It propagates our loneliness
We're all the same in that way

Did she think I was upset with her when I was stressed and frustrated
with myself?
When I told her I needed some space?
And she didn't respect that...

She doesn't like me
She thinks I treated her badly
And now I'm thinking about people that have treated me badly
For no reason
Strangers
Bosses

Speaking loudly
Or aggressively
About how wrong I am
About my tone

And they don't listen
They don't realize how inappropriate they're being
How rude
How inconsiderate

And when I told her I don't like loud voices
She said well my voice got loud too

The Roommate

She throws out my chicken
She throws out my art
She throws out recycling
But she never throws out the trash

Her girlfriend lived with us for 3 months

    no rent, not on lease

I can't pay the last 2 months

    and I get stuck

She's passive aggressive
She thinks it's funny

    or healthy

I tell her I need her to communicate things to me

    she doesn't

I don't clean enough for her

    because I won't clean up her mess

She doesn't load the dishwasher with her dishes

    She doesn't unload it either

She makes fun of my trauma

She makes guilting comments

    If I stay up late or get up early

She doesn't tell me people are coming over on my work night
She says she's getting a dog

    Not to specify it's a puppy

Missing You, or Grief, Now Acceptance

I've been having dreams of yearning

    For you
    For loving supportive parents

I cry in them

I know I was the one that went away
In a move of total self isolation
But it feels like I've been abandoned

I miss you all so much
You all were my support system
It was you I called when I was about to attempt suicide

    (I still did)

You and your partner always loved and cared about me
You were both so understanding in my mental breakdown
When I needed to talk about my trauma
You both were always so excited to see me after we hadn't seen each
other for a time

It feels like you have all moved on

    Without me
    From me

You've all graduated

It looks like you all have successful fulfilling lives on social media
I know you're working on your master's degree
At Stanford fucking University

What have I been doing the last 5 years?
Working dead end jobs
And relying on my abusive parents for most of my social interactions
I miss my community so much
I worked so hard for it
But so much time has passed
You're all living in different cities anyway

I want to know your thoughts on different tv shows and movies
On social and political events
On my trauma and recovery
I want to hear about your life,

        Your recovery

I want to know how Adian is doing
I want to know if I've finally spelled their name correctly

I wish your partner would talk to me
I wish we could hold a conversation

Has too much time passed?

It's like there is a crater in my life
Where love used to be
And I can't fill it with new relationships
Because they love different

I want your life
I want your loving and supportive parents
I want your loving and supportive partner
I want your friends
I want your career that you love

I don't really want them
And I know you have trauma too
But they are things I wish I could have

I've seen your new fat non-binary friend on Instagram
I know they came to visit you in California
I know you met them in Chicago after I left
It feels like you replaced me

I wondered last night if I had asked you out
Before you met Adian
If you would still be in my life

I imagine our relationship would probably have been worse
I might not have been able to call you when I was suicidal
I was thinking about how I've been having dreams yearning for our
friendship
Eating a banana for breakfast
The morning after the second dream about you
A few minutes after I had messaged you saying
I wish I had known you were in New York,
I would have invited you to see me

And I start to cry for the first time in years

Untitled

What my gender is today
Won't be what it is tomorrow
How I dress
How I feel
What I say
Is ever changing
Developing
Into something new
Or something old refinished

My closet is enormous
I have clothes for every occasion of gender
Every season
Every event
I might need to present differently
I might be feeling differently

My clothes are precious
They reflect how I feel
They shape how others feel about me

My jewelry is overflowing
The most commonly worn pieces sit in a pile on my dresser
Like a dragon's horde
And like the miserly creature I admire the shine and sparkle
Unlike the dragon I use my gems and treasures
And put them back later to be used again

Accidents

I feel so ashamed
I feel like a child
I wish I could go home

    and change
    and shower

At least no one else is at work and can smell the pee
But now I have to work in these damp clothes for hours
I should've asked for Gigi to stay so I could go pee
Instead I'm alone with soaked pants
It should be mostly dry by the time Jenniset comes in
All I can do is hope she doesn't smell it

I'm not sure this bladder retraining thing is working
I'm having accidents

    small ones
    (not usually as big as this)

Do I need adult diapers?

    Like the child I am

Other people's experiences can't possibly be like this
And I won't be able to see another pelvic floor physical therapist till
June

Urinary Incontinence aka Pee Problems

Walk a mile in my shoes
and you'll have to change your underwear
I seriously can't go a day without getting damp

I can't exactly *feel* it happening
But I can feel the results

I feel the frustration

> the shame
> the confusion
> the humor
> the annoyance

I went to the bathroom 2 hours ago
and according to my "Bladder Training"
I'm supposed to wait longer

> In my wet panties

But here I go again to pee

> Always to pee
> I've spent my life consumed by where I'll pee
> NOT to mention which bathroom I can pee in

I can't keep it in
My muscles are weak
My muscles are overactive
It's stress

It's urge
It's mixed

I'm doing the stretches
Why isn't this working
Why can't I go a whole day without getting damp underwear

Did they even finish potty training me
Is that what this is

P. S.

THERE WASN'T EVEN THAT MUCH PEE!!!

why couldn't you fucking hold it in (*seething directed at Mr. Bladder)

Pee Schedule

Peeing every 2 hours
god what a joke

"Bladder Retraining" got me peeing like 10 times a day

Now I'm sitting here trying not to pee my pants
because my 2 hours is 40 minutes up
and my roommate decided to take a bath without telling me

The **entire** reason to do this was to avoid peeing my pants
and yet here we are
barely able to contain myself

The Year That Never Ended

How many summers have passed since this started
How many "the most important election of our lifetimes" have there been
How many times has the president said this was over
How many shots have I gotten now
How many times have I heard people say that it's all fake
How many times have I put on my mask before I face the world
How many times have I had to change the type of mask I wear
How many times has this thing mutated
How many times will we see another passing
How many times have I wanted to scream and yell and cry at our losses
How many 9/11s a day will we have
How many of us won't get our taste back
How many more?

    (indignant, enraged)

How many more

    (depressed, resigned)

How many times will we be told that it's over?

That Time I Almost Died

Every day since January I had been taking my gender euphoria pills.
I hadn't bled since February
Sprintec was such a gift.

By June my hormones had given me clots all over both my lungs.
For weeks I was at home
not having seen a face I didn't live with
since March.
That pride month I should've been out in the streets
instead I could barely climb the stairs.

I woke up in the middle of the night
I couldn't breathe.
I couldn't calm my heartbeat
for hours.
I waited until my father returned from third shift at the grocery.
He woke my mother.
They drove me to the emergency room in my spiderman pajamas.

I needed a wheelchair
I needed a COVID test
I needed a CAT scan
I needed an ultrasound
I needed to stop my birth control immediately

I spent my first day in the ICU
Transported by medical professionals in radiation resistant suits
with faces, hair, eyes, hands, arms, legs, feet
all encased in plastic.

I didn't touch another human's skin for a week.

When my ICU doctor asked how I spend my weekends
I said I didn't do much.
He was surprised,
"Really, you're so young, you should go out more!"
I stared at him over my face mask.
"We're in quarantine."
He laughed.
He had forgotten,
Hazmat lookin suit and all.

Juneteenth and Father's Day were the same weekend that year.
I drifted in and out of sleep while Black Panther, Atlanta,
and a Dinosaur Train Father's Day special
played on my empty room's TV.
In my dreams I thought I was bound to the bed.
In reality I was hooked up to so many wires.

When my Heparin drip had thinned my blood enough
they wheeled me to the Heart Wing
with many patients recovering from COVID.
I couldn't move in bed without having to catch my breath
I wasn't allowed to get out of bed
Have you had to use a bedpan before?
I couldn't poop for 5 days.
I don't find jokes about them funny anymore
It's degrading to the user and the helper

I was given wipes, deodorant, a comb, a toothbrush
all out of reach to me on the windowsill.
It wasn't until midweek someone told me

I could comb my hair with their awful thin tooth comb.

I couldn't see anyone, not in my COVID recovery unit.
I was 23 and so grateful not to be dead or dying.
By the end of the week I was menstruating again
and much to my horror
it was the most comically heavy and clotted flow I have ever had.
They could only give me pads.
Thankfully I could use the toilet at that point.
When I asked the doctor about how I shouldn't be having any clots
he laughed with embarrassment and simply said
"Menstrual blood works differently.
Eliquis is probably going to make it heavier."

My first ER doctor, finishing up his residency,
and my last nurse who got me discharged
were the only remotely transgender competent providers I had met.
I begged the nurses to help me with the birth control
I couldn't go back to the horror I was living.
It was my last day they talked to me
about making me an appointment.

All week I would lay there
getting my blood taken every few hours,
even in the middle of the night.
I would read on my phone mostly or
I would look out my window thinking
of those I had seen in the streets
of those I had seen being taken off the streets in unmarked vans
of those I had seen protesting lockdown
of how I couldn't breathe
of how George Floyd couldn't breathe

of how people were chanting his final words
of how people all over my hospital couldn't breathe
of how people all over my state, my country, my continent, my world
couldn't breathe

It was a time when we all realized what we needed most to live.

The Toilet
The sacred space!
Burst open for all to see!

My little room of ruminations
My closet for hiding
The bowl I flush my tears away in

But the door!

The portcullis of my fortress

Betrayed me!
Left me vulnerable and defenseless
Viewed by the masses!

Shock!
Outage!
Confusion!

How could someone have burst through my defenses?
Will this happen again?

Toilet feelings
Toilet feelings
Toilet feelings

The cuts weren't finished clotting and now I'll have to try to get my blood out of my jeans when I go home.

Or I could just have bloody jeans now. They're black. That's pretty punk.

Damnit I shouldn't've leaned forward to pee. Now there's blood on my arm.

Just a little treat before having to go out again. To therapy. Just a few cuts.

I was supposed to hold this pee for 2 hours and I couldn't hold it 20 minutes.

Ironic I'm wearing a pad that's full of pee and pants that's full of blood.

I wish I could talk to someone about the cutting
But I'm so glad it's a secret

I'm wearing shorts
I'm wearing a bathing suit
My arm is tanned

     the markings white against the browner skin

Do they see it?
Do they think they're old?
My leg is red and ingrained, not six months old
My arm is white and raised, five years old
Why don't they say anything?

I wish I could speak of them
Explain
I wish I could've explained to them while it was happening

They see the scrapes on my knees and arms
But do they see the scars?

In the toilet

    again

First date

    nervous
    hiding

I'm on time
She's late

She asked if she could stay the night
In case she drinks too much

A little presumptuous on the first date
Not a great sign that she's *planning* on getting wasted on a first date

We'll see how this goes

Sitting at the table
Wishing I had thought to order wine

She says she's coming in
Do we shake hands?

    (I would prefer)

Do we hug?

She'll be right in

WRONG
WRONG
WRONG

Why did you touch me
Why did you kiss me
Why did I let you

Why didn't I tell you what I was feeling
Why did I just want to be nice
Why did your gift giving have to make me feel special
Why did it have to make me feel taken care of

Why are you trying to make an instant relationship
Why are you over sharing
Why did you caress my leg
Why did you have to use gender slurs

Why
Why
Why

Why do I put myself in these situations
Why do I let men take control of me without my consent
Why am I tempted to let him suck me into this relationship he's already
created in his head
Why do I feel like he's going to steal that special thing that makes me
me

How do I make my lips my own again

Are you knocking at my door?

Is it still a breakup if we weren't technically dating?

"You've already been through so much
I don't want to put you through more"

A mutual parting
We need different things
We'll still be friends

Trying to find someone is so difficult
Putting yourself out there isn't a one time thing
It's constantly making yourself vulnerable
Over and over again
Only to be disappointed

The pool is already small
You have to like them
They have to like you
It gets smaller when you consider that I'm

    Fat
    Trans
    Non-binary
    Neurodivergent
    Communist

Now I have to consider that I'm traumatized?

It feels like I'm damaged

But it's more likely that I'm delicate
That I need to be treated with care

After everything he did to me

    that *they* did to me

I want to have fun
I want to experiment

But I have to sit around and wait

    not for a savior
    as much as I might want one

For a compatible companion
And sift through assholes and transphobes on dating sites
For the next 2-3 years until my time comes around again

Who's to Blame?

I don't feel good today
I have so many Toilet Feelings
But it's not my fault
And it's not his fault either
But since it's not his fault
It feels like it's mine

I'm so used to making excuses for other people

    Especially men

For why it isn't their fault

    He's depressed
    He's autistic
    He's schizophrenic
    She's in an abusive relationship

Then there are those who have no excuse
But somehow it's still my fault

I feel like I've failed
Like I'm bad for having needs
For being delicate
He knew what I needed before I did
It's why he pulled away

Did my trauma scare him away?
Did it trigger him?
How can I get someone to stay when I'm so damaged?

Vomit

Vomit
Vomit
Vomit

It's not even that something is wrong

    (I'm wrong)

I've got nothing to be upset about
My mind is speeding through these shitty thoughts

    Of how I'm shitty

(Crying)
Why is my mind built this way?

    Do you ever wanna...

Throw up
Throw up
Throw up

THROW UP
THROW UP

It's that my anxiety over things

    I have done
    Will do

Have thought of doing

Fill my stomach up with doubts and shame
It bubbles up
And up
And up
And up

It's ironic that these
Toilet Feelings
are making me nauseous

What do others think of me?
Why don't I feel good?
Bad
Bad
Bad

God
I'm so ugly
That was a pretty cruel choice
To make me fucking ugly
But you must've always hated me
Everything else in my life has sucked
Maybe I am demon spawn

Stress
Stress
Stress

Someone didn't show up
Someone quit yesterday
The only other person can't come in

People keep coming in wave after wave
There's no stop to the work
I don't have enough hands
I don't have enough mouths
To please the masses by myself

There's 4 more hours and my feet already hurt

Oh my god
I'm in so much pain
Why did I wear these goddamn shoes

Bread for all, and Roses too

There's things I want
Things I need
Things that I deserve
Things that everyone deserves
If they want them

But I cannot have
I try to make up for these things
By replacing them with others
By stealing from work
By eating comfort foods
By writing poetry

I want to be fulfilled
I want to be able to pay rent

    And take a paid week off once a year

I want to know what to do with my life
I want to finish school
I want to make art
I want meaningful relationships

Alas they remain unreachable

How silly of me to have an emotional reaction to a stressful situation
How naive of me to think this situation is unusual
How dumb of me to share it

I'm new and I'm stressed and I don't know what's going on and I've been abandoned
And you're telling me this happens everywhere?
So this is normal
So I shouldn't be feeling this way

Our experiences are not the same
Mine did not prepare me for this
You just dismissed me
They laughed at me
It's a feeling
Why are you belittling me for a feeling?

There's nothing I want to say
I'm dragged down
My body is in pain
My clothes don't work
I'm sad
I'm exhausted
I don't know what I'm doing
I'm encouraged to do more
Burnout is on the horizon

Lunch Break

You make me feel bad
I'm in a bad mood
There's so much to do
And I'm doing my best
And somehow I'm not doing enough

I didn't like your passive aggressive comment
Or that you spilled my coffee
Or you speaking over the person that was helping me spell "availability"
So like an idiot I have to ask her to spell it again

It's not that you're a lot
It's that I feel like you're not aware of your environment
Like I'm not so much ignored
As other people generally aren't taken into consideration

You're telling me to do something a certain way
In a not very nice way
But I know you didn't do something correctly last night!
So why should I trust what you're saying

You even said that no one trained you
That you don't know policies
So I don't appreciate what you said

And I'm spending my break feeling shitty
Taking a break *from you*

The wifi is terrible at work
I guess it's another toilet session distractionless

Performance Theatre

I did the song and dance
I performed like the circus monkey
But it wasn't good enough

When we met I did it perfectly

    And she was just as unresponsive
    Giving me nothing to work with

When she decided to show me a perfect performance
Her actress was the girl she just hired
And treated the real customers
Just as I had treated her moments before

Her performance was exceptional

    With a willing participant
    (something she didn't allot me)

Her performance was abysmal

    Outside of her fiction she did exactly what I did wrong from
    the stage

I won't get the monkey's job
My improv partner set me up for failure

I still did better than she did when it mattered

How will I make rent next month?

Mirror Image

All this time in the mirror
And I don't know who's looking back at me
That's not my face
That's not my body
That's not my hair
Who is this person?

I stared into their eyes
I looked at the shape of their curves
I watched them move
But they do not look familiar

Perhaps it's someone that I saw from work
Sat near on the bus
Passed at the grocery store
But I don't know them

They have acne
And a double chin
And patchy eyebrows
And their hourglass looks more pear shaped with their tummy and
saggy tits

At night during the dinner party

    Warm lighting

The men and women pass around their face
Trying it on

Laughing
Speaking in a voice not their own
Mice leave my mouth as I try to speak
The face always ends up with me

What is it to see yourself truly?

Perceptions of the Self

When I look in the mirror I don't know who I see

But it's different from when I was younger
I didn't know who I was
And it plagued me

Now I look older
And fatter

Neither of which are bad things
They were inevitable

But I don't know this face
Or this body

Am I presenting myself in a way that's what I want?
Do I just need to cut my hair?

I don't feel at home in my body

I try to wear clothes that make me happy
But are they making me happy or do I like the way they look?
Are they affirming my gender or do I appreciate the aesthetic?

Your gender is whatever you want it to be
My body doesn't reflect what I want my gender to be

Dressed up my body still feels strange

But I look perfect

Is that me?

Refrigerator Magnet

A magnet
Once a fantasy
Then a promise, a goal
For a short time, reality. The blessed truth
A fall
Into a dark crevice full of monsters new and old

A promise again
Now a regret

Have I peaked?
Oh my god

Fat body
Deformed body
Trying to kill me body
Can't see body
Mentally ill body
Trash body
Two sizes too big body
Non cancerous tumor body
Clots in my lungs body

piece of shit piece of shit piece of shit
Am I a toilet
Or do I belong in one?
a little fat crying pile of poop

I wanna throw up
I wanna die
I wanna bleed and bleed and cry

i wanna die i wanna die i wanna die i wanna die i wanna die i wanna die
i wanna die i wanna die i wanna die i wanna die i wanna die i wanna die
i wanna die i wanna die i wanna die i wanna die i wanna die i wanna die
i wanna die i wanna die i wanna die i wanna die i wanna die i wanna die
i wanna die i wanna die i wanna die i wanna die i wanna die i wanna die
i wanna die i wanna die i wanna die i wanna die i wanna die i wanna die
i wanna die i wanna die i wanna die i wanna die i wanna die i wanna die
i wanna die i wanna die i wanna die i wanna die i wanna die i wanna die

Bad
And dark
And shoulders slumped

I take a break from the world
Only to have it creep in on me
Telling me I'm unworthy

Hate
Hate
Hate
Bad
Bad
Bad

Why are you so ugly?
Why are you so fat?

You're such a waste
You're so dumb
And you're gonna sing a silly little song while you wash your hands?
Idiot

s p a c e d. o u t.°.*

Ugh
Bathroom break making me need a break

I'm so sick of these Toilet Feelings
Who ever heard of a toilet having feelings?

I'm ready to lose that which is attached to me

    The memories
    The events
    The relationships

That have hurt me

And just fade into the universe
All that pain won't belong to anyone
I'll be free
I'll be everything

An Evening Spacewalk

The universe is full of

    Love
    Hate
    Joy
    Sadness

No

The universe is everything
The universe is nothing
There are no feelings

As I lay myself down for sleep and I seep into my mattress
I find the barriers between myself and the universe fade
I'm a quantum compared to the universe
But I'm made of the same stuff stars are

I breathe in I'm nothing
I breathe out I'm everything

I've got my oxygen on and I'm ready for my space walk
Ready to enter into

    The abyss
    The everything
    My dreams

Another Hour Passed

An entire year has slipped through my fingers
and there's no getting it back

My twenties lost to

    covid
    depression
    isolation
    recovery

I want my time of

    recklessness
    fucking
    partying
    community
    back

I want to throw up
I want to cry
I want to cut my skin and die

I thought I had another year
I thought I had more time

But
The clock wasn't supposed to have this many hours
How can I ask for more time?

Kaleb,

It's been a while since we spoke
You've left me on read
Again and again

A lot has changed
My life is so different
I'm so different
Yet I know you would recognize me immediately

Four years ago my life collapsed
I was in vertigo
We weren't fair weather friends
You saw me through it
But you belittled me as well

You were suffering and grieving
But so was I
And my ego was dying

I can't blame you
For not knowing how to handle my breakdown
Or my flashbacks

We were so young

But you were cruel

You lacked compassion
You didn't value our friendship the way I did
You didn't love me the way I did
Because love is for losers

And when someone much too young for you treated you the same
I had to baby you
Listen to you try not to cry
And watch you drink wine right out of the box wine bag

I used to write my poetry to you
But now I imagine if you read them
It would be too much

    Too much feelings
    Too much honesty
    Too much me

I *imagine* you would push me away.
Like regular you

Not Okay

You used to say such terrible things about me,
now they come with much less frequency
and usually with a laugh.

But there are so many things I want to say to you

    about how you harmed me
    (Ruined me)

I want to tell you about the work I've had to put into this

    Because of you

I want to yell
more than I used to
and more purposefully,
better articulated.
Because now I know what you were doing
Was wrong

And you think we're fine now
Everything's okay!

I'm not okay

You made me not okay

You would yell
And hit
And go on about your troubles

And I would stay quiet

    Otherwise I'd get hit
    Or yelled at more strongly

Now people go on about their issues

    (Inappropriate for a stranger
    Or coworker)

They get close to me

    Too close
    (Aggressive sometimes)

Occasionally they touch me

    When I do not want to be touched
    When I do not ask to be touched
    When I do not consent to be touched
    (Sexually too)

But people love to yell

    About the most preposterous things
    You're unable to control your anger over *that*?

(Sometimes they say they're not angry, and boy, isn't *that* a
trigger?)

I don't really fight it
I try to make it pass by letting the person step all over me
Appeasing them

(Using me)

Or I freeze up
And wait until the situation dissolves

The most simple things can cause this response
Someone speaking loudly and negatively

But not yelling

Someone simply being upset
And handling it well

And I'm staying up tonight to write this down

Because I'm such a *sensitive person*
Because people's *words and tone affect how I feel*

The woman today is just an aggressive person
Maybe she wasn't angry
But she was yelling

(Angrily)
(Condescendingly)

I'll internalize when someone is upset about something entirely unrelated to me
And is angrily complaining about it
Because somehow her dad being shitty is my fault
Because somehow the coordinator telling me to give you something on your break is my fault
Because the traffic is my fault

You made me feel like everything was my fault!

Anticipation

I've started thinking about how I would eulogize you

I image myself at a pulpit

    (The only way to get me into a church is for weddings and
    funerals)

Probably at your parish of twenty years
Above the basement where I was first sexually assaulted
And I get to share with your family what you did to me
Since I can't at Thanksgiving.

It started with a typical night with mom,
hanging out, watching tv,
Then you come downstairs
With those loud oppressive steps
That I associate with your incidents of anger
And I was so filled with dread that you were coming downstairs
That I imagined what if you never came downstairs again

What relief it brought!
Never to be put through this again!

    The only fear,
    Pain,
    Voice I would hear,

Would be memories.

I'm already haunted today by the things you've done to me,

So I know your death won't change anything.
And I'm sure I'll grieve you
And mourn
And cry like a baby

    (That you let cry itself hoarse after a day and a half)

But your reign of terror will be over
There is no more pain you could create in your death

And in the absence of mourning,
I hope for the freedom of your terror
And the freedom to share what you've done.
I anticipate the time in which I can have our family be just as confused
about how they should feel about your passing as I feel

I want them to have the confusion of memories of

    Yelling
    Laughing
    Hitting
    Hugs

I want to save my mother from his wrath

    (From their codependency)

I want her to understand what he did was wrong
What she did was wrong
What she did for him was wrong

But she'll never understand

She'll never come to terms.

I can't be alone in this
I can't be the only one

Family Portrait

All six of us
in blues and grays and whites
My mother and father standing on either sides of my older brothers
My younger brother and I seated
My father and younger brother, clean faced
My older brothers in their beards

The eldest is to the right in a button up shirt, likely plaid, slacks, and
with one eyebrow quirked

>   His hair is short and dark, curly, and parted to his right

>   His beard is full but short, length at the bottom of the chin
>   but cut closely at the cheeks

>   His face has little color but full cheeks

The second eldest is to the left and also in a button up shirt, this one
flannel, jeans, and his glasses

>   His hair is also dark and short, hairline receding from stress,
>   there is no wave to his hair at this length

>   His beard is mid length, wavy, and in normal lighting it is
>   red, in this color pallet it is much lighter than the hair on the
>   top of his head

>   He has lines on his face, in his brow, on his cheeks, but there
>   is much color to his face

The youngest is seated on the left, wearing his favorite sweater, a Christmas gift from myself, color blocked and ribbed. He is wearing jeans and his glasses as always

His hair is mid dark and shaped like my father's: short and wavy, parted to his right

At 18, he has no beard to speak of but we shall see what will develop

He does not have lines in his youthful face and he has some color to his cheeks. His eyebrows are particularly bushy, which I am jealous of

My father is on the far left and he is wearing a button up shirt and slacks with a dark belt. He smiling

His hair is lighter than the rest of us but there are some grays creeping in. Though the viewer cannot see it, there is a spot that is thinning in the back. He parts it to the right and in his older years his hair waves more easily the longer it gets

Unlike his younger years, his face is clean shaven

His face is lined, you can see them better with his smile. His eyes are light. Unlike the rest of us

He is holding gardening shears, elbow bent

My mother is to the far right, the shortest, she is wearing a black dress, modest cut, a little too long on her short arms and legs

Her hair goes to her mid breast or to her shoulder. It is dark naturally with some grays coming through. It is thick

She has peach fuzz on her chin which has become darker
and more pronounced with age

She has lines on her face. At her brow and her eyes. At her
mouth

She is wearing makeup creating artificial color in her cheeks

She is holding weed killer with both hands. She is not
smiling

I am seated next to my younger brother, on the left.
I am flowers
The only color in the portrait are the blooms of my body
My face and torso and legs and arms and hands
Are all made of chrysanthemums and daisies and roses and violets and
every flower you can think of

It is signed with my first initial and last name
In red

I lost my childhood to you

I lost my childhood to you
To this
This terror
This bullshit

And there's no amount of reparenting
Or soothing the inner child
That will fill that hole
Where love from one's parents is supposed to be

It's supposed to soothe the pain,
Make it more manageable
But living with the perpetrators of this horror makes it difficult to do
that work

    (they undermined me, made me rely on them so they could
    hurt me, making it impossible to work on independence)

But never in my childhood was I truly happy
My earliest memories I can identify adolescent depression
I was alone or being tortured
I was neglected or being starved

    (Being hit)

I struggle so much now due to what you did to me then
I don't know how to reach happiness because of how you woefully
unprepared me

>How you denied my childhood depression

I know I can reach happiness away from you
But you've made me strung to you and I need help to cut the umbilical cord

You made me miserable as a child
Yet it is you who called me a miserable child
My most important years of development

>Gone
>Never coming back
>Abandoned
>(Like me)

I deserved to have years of joy

>Of laughter
>Of love
>Of learning

You never nurtured me

>Emotionally
>Intellectually
>Physically

You've hurt me so deeply and meaningfully that I struggle with

>Relationships
>Friendships
>Second dates
>Chatting online

Flirting
Bosses
Food
Eating as a comfort
Avoiding eating
Starving myself
Work
Fawning at authority
Being walked all over
Being forced into tasks I don't want or can't do
Being abused
Executive Functioning
Not knowing how to brush my teeth
Or tie my shoes
Not going to the doctor
Or going to the bathroom when I need to
And more

When I was 5, I decided at Christmas I didn't believe in God
It didn't seem logical to me
Through that train of thought
I realized Santa Claus, the Easter Bunny, and sadly, the Tooth Fairy
weren't real either
I was so young and you made me believe the world was so dark and cold

     That I was so unlovable

You stole the magic of my youth

I loved stories of magic
Of hurt children finding loving families
But I wasn't Matilda or Cosette or Harry
CPS never took me away or sent you to parenting classes

There are no dragons and I have no magic powers

    I've tried

I always thought I was more like the Baudelaire's
But they had once been happy
And were supportive of each other

I had found my family once and you took me from them
This isn't a sad chapter in an uplifting book
This is a happier chapter in a sad book
Because you've stopped the torture

    (Mostly)

And I'm trying to get away

    (Again)

You took away something precious
And made it something awful
I stole away inside my head
In daydreams where I was still tortured,
But by real villains,
Ones I can fight
And become a triumphant hero
Because I was so sick I couldn't imagine myself as happy

LANTA isn't public transit, obviously

Another bus ride
Hopefully you won't miss your connection

    like this morning
    when you cried

The guy behind you is on the phone and complaining how the 319 now stops at the airport (which is dumb) and no longer goes to ATC

You want to say it's because your line, the 105, no longer goes to the mall so now you have to connect to a line that doesn't run late or on weekends at the airport (which *is* dumb)

What used to be a 15 minute commute is now an hour and a half

If you're lucky

Today you left at 11:30 and didn't get to work till 1:15 because while you were early the bus was late. Twice.

And now at night it's the last bus of the night so you better not miss your connection

The 105 driver towards the airport likes to stop at fucking Wawa though in the middle of the trip and you just want to go home. And when you want coffee at work you bring a fucking thermos. You know the drivers are allowed to have food and drink with them

You're so close to making a complaint

As you pass onto the tilghman street bridge you have to pass the anti choice billboard which is very attractive looking with a very cute baby so it's hard not to look at when you're not driving

And you get so angry

You want to scream, stab the advertisement, move to Vermont where billboards are illegal, tear it down, burn it, scream some more

But instead you fight off tears

You've made it to BTC waiting for the 105 but it's not on the fucking LANTAbus map app so god knows where it is

You feel good walking home while there's lightning in the clouds

oh god it's the guy that stops for coffee

Now you pass the school you cried at earlier today while you waited for someone to pick you up out of the 100° heat that you burned in

They demolished the 100 year old school that you went to. The one that had asbestos falling from the ceiling. It used to be where the new football field is now. It looks like a college now

There he goes, adding several minutes onto your trip. Gotta get that Wawa coffee fix

Police at the grocery store. Thank god they're not there for you

You said thank you to him and feel dumb

Home. Finally

Toilet feelings
Toilet feelings
Toilet feelings

God you're dumb
Why did you say that
You think you're smart or some shit
You think you have something worth sharing

Bad
Bad
Bad

Shut up
Stay home
Shield yourself

It's not worth it

Do you ever feel...

bad?

Like you're bad
Like nothing good can come of you
Like you'll always be bad
Like this world is bad and is made to churn out more bad people
Like everyone knows you're bad

Do you ever feel...

like trash?

Like deep fried garbage
Like you'll never get clean
Like everyone is piling on more trash and one day you'll just be a barge
out in the ocean

Do you ever feel...

like a piece of shit?

Like you're not worth anything
Like no one loves you

Like you don't deserve love
Like you're a perverted unholy heretic that's been cast out of society

Do you ever feel...

　　　like crying?

Like tears should be streaming down your face
Like your chest should be heaving, your mouth should be blubbering
Like you're absolutely miserable and you should be sobbing for hours
night and day but you can't

Do you ever feel...

　　　like vomit?

Like you've been rejected
Like you're undigested
Like you'll never be digested
Like you'll be flushed away
Like instead of being born into this world you were the result of your
mother's unfortunate indigestion

Do you ever feel...

　　　dead?

Like your body is decomposing
Like your life has ended

Like nothing matters
Like nothing affects you
Like if you were cut you wouldn't bleed
Like your soul has left your body and you're walking around without
thoughts or feelings

Do you ever feel...

bad?

I've made a huge mistake

So now your poem has become an intrusive thought
What was supposed to be a cathartic coping mechanism for depression
and anxiety has now become the fuel for them

This is hell

It's a good poem

    (maybe)

And I like sharing it

But I can't really think on it myself because otherwise...

Do you ever feel...

*like a plastic bag, drifting through the wind, wanting to start
again*

Do you ever feel

feel so paper thin, like a house of cards, one blow from cavin in

Katy Perry helps I guess
Sometimes it makes me smile

It's ridiculous is what it is

"like a piece of shit" and "like a plastic bag"
Same syllables, same cadence

This was unintentional

It began as coincidence
But now I use it to thought stop
Because it doesn't feel particularly good to wallow in piece of shitiness

So now whenever it comes to mind
You just gotta ignite the light
And let it shine
Just own the night
Like the Fourth of July

Cause baby, you're a firework
Come on, show 'em what you're worth

I need to be gentle with myself
Unemployed for the second time in less than 6 months
It's difficult not to feel like a failure

I have no control over the economy
It's not my fault
I did everything right

There has to be a cosmic reason why
I can't possibly be this unlucky for fun

Maybe I'll get a job for 2 months and move to a new city

There's nothing to say
there's just these Toilet Feelings

This life I've carved out for myself

    this home

The shallow little bowl of my life
Connected to hundreds of others by pipes
Someone else sends down "flushable" wipes and tampons
And now my little home reeks

We all have our own little bowls
Separated by walls and doors
To create a veneer of privacy.

    Because I can still hear you when you pee

Everyone must experience these Toilet Feelings
in their own bowls
Why don't they experience it the way I do?
Do they simply not show it?
Is it because my Pee Pee Problems send me to the toilet more
frequently?

Why did we have to clog the fucking sewer?
Now I can't breathe

Don't miss out!

Visit the website below and you can sign up to receive emails whenever Igoe Brown publishes a new book. There's no charge and no obligation.

https://books2read.com/r/B-A-PEIYB-BPZIF

BOOKS2READ

Connecting independent readers to independent writers.

Did you love *Toilet Feelings*? Then you should read *Bummer Summer*[1] by Igoe Brown!

You ever had a bad summer? A sad summer? A heartbroken summer full of upheaval? Igoe Brown's last summer began with a sexual assault, followed by social fallout, and ended with new relationships. Join them on their journey of healing through poetry during a summer of sorrows and restoration.

---

1. https://books2read.com/u/meaRgz

2. https://books2read.com/u/meaRgz

About the Author

Brown currently lives in Pennsylvania writing away their anxieties in a politically and literally turbulent climate.

www.ingramcontent.com/pod-product-compliance
Lightning Source LLC
Chambersburg PA
CBHW022008170726

47994CB00023B/2432